GW01019516

BIBLE
HEROES

My book about being
a **hero** for God

by Nick Harding

Copyright © Nick Harding 2011
First published 2011
ISBN 978 1 84427 579 3

Scripture Union
207–209 Queensway, Bletchley, Milton Keynes, MK2 2EB
Email: info@scriptureunion.org.uk
Website: www.scriptureunion.org.uk

Scripture Union Australia
Locked Bag 2, Central Coast Business Centre, NSW 2252
Website: www.scriptureunion.org.au

Scripture Union USA
PO Box 987, Valley Forge, PA 19482
Website: www.scriptureunion.org

All rights reserved. No part of this publication may be reproduced, stored in a retrieval system, or transmitted in any form or by any means, electronic, mechanical, photocopying, recording or otherwise, without the prior permission of Scripture Union.

The right of Nick Harding to be identified as the author of this work has been asserted by her in accordance with the Copyright, Designs and Patents Act 1988.

Scripture quotations are from the Contemporary English Version © American Bible Society 1991, 1992, 1995. Anglicisations © British and Foreign Bible Society 1996. Published in the UK by HarperCollinsPublishers and used with permission.

British Library Cataloguing-in-Publication Data
A catalogue record of this book is available from the British Library.

Printed and bound in China by 1010 Printing International Ltd.
Cover and internal design: kwgraphicdesign
Illustrations by Sean Parkes

↳ Scripture Union is an international charity working with churches in more than 130 countries, providing resources to bring the good news of Jesus Christ to children, young people and families and to encourage them to develop spiritually through the Bible and prayer.

As well as our network of volunteers, staff and associates who run holidays, church-based events and school Christian groups, we produce a wide range of publications and support those who use our resources through training programmes.

Contents

Who is a hero?

Who is your hero? Here are some suggestions – circle the ones that are heroes to you, and add some others too:

My dad

Racing drivers

Grandad

Footballers

Brother

Pop stars

Friend

Youth leader

Rugby stars

Why do people become heroes? I think it's because they do things that are out-of-the ordinary, wonderful, life-changing, and really good for other people. TV shows make "stars" of lots of people, but they've not all got loads of talent and aren't really heroes at all. A hero is something special....

The Bible is full of real-life boys and men who were heroes. Some stood up bravely for what was right, and others fought for God. Some were great warriors, and others spoke out against all the powerful people of the time. They all lived differently, and didn't simply go along with the crowd. The thing I love most about these boys and men who were heroes is that (almost) none of them were perfect. They made mistakes, they lost their confidence, they failed...but they're still heroes for God!

These real guys have heaps to tell us about how we should live, and it's worth thinking about each one really carefully. So go on and read on. Each hero has a TOTAL HERO RATING, SO YOU CAN CHECK OUT who is the Top Hero for doing God's stuff, age, generosity and strength. Compare them, and see whether you agree.

If you were going to be remembered as a hero in 200 years' time, what would you like to be remembered for?

So read on, have a think about these **Bible heroes**, and see whether you think you match up. Your mission, should you wish to take it, is to find out about God's heroes, and become one of his heroes yourself!

We remember him because...

Adam

In the beginning...

BACKGROUND BIT

Place	Garden of Eden and the fields around it
When	At the beginning of time
Job	Look after God's fantastic world
Key bit	"The Lord made a garden in a place called Eden, which was in the east, and he put the man there." *Genesis 2:8*
Other guys	Eve, the snake (hisssss!), sons, God

God created "man" and all the other animals. Have a go at drawing and naming a new kind of animal... completely your own invention.

Adam is the first man in the Bible... and wasn't ever a boy! God made Adam at the same time as he created the world and everything in it. Turn over for the first bit of his story...

God had been busy – he had made a really great world, perfect in every way. He had created animals and plants, sorted out night and day, separated land and water, and now it was ready. So God decided to make a man – a different sort of animal. This first human, Adam, was given power over the animals and birds, gave them their names, and lived in peace. The only rule was that he mustn't eat the fruit from one particular tree...peasy! Then God made a woman, a female human to keep Adam company...

I like her!

I like him!

This is our special garden.

Go on, Eve, try the fruit of the special tree. No one will know....

Adam, try this fruit from that tree. I know what God said, but it's got a great taste.

What's going on in my head? I knew it was wrong to eat that fruit...what have we done?

You know that feeling in the pit of your tummy when you just know that things are going to get really bad, like when you answer back at home, or get caught out at school....

What happened next?

- God was really angry that Adam and Eve had eaten the fruit.
- He sent them out of the lovely garden.
- Adam continued to be a hero – he looked after Eve, had three children that started the human race growing, and grew food.
- But things were never quite the same.

Have a look at the two pictures opposite of what that wonderful Garden of Eden could have looked like. There are 11 things different – how many can you spot?

How much hero?

Length of life
930 years (but years may have been
counted in a different way then!) **100%**

Family
Wife: Eve
Children: Cain, Abel, Seth **80%**

Amazing moments
Being made, seeing Eve,
eating that bad fruit **80%**

Doing God's stuff
Great, but then it all went wrong **50%**

Generosity
God's friend, shared with Eve **65%**

Strength
Gave in to temptation way too easily **30%**

TOTAL HERO RATING **67.5%**

Find out more about Adam in the Bible
– great stuff in Genesis 1 through to the
end of Genesis 5.

So there we go – Adam made a
rubbish choice to eat the fruit,
and things didn't go so well from
then on. He was a hero...but
one who made a big mistake by
being tempted and giving way.

There are tons of things that can
tempt us, and when we give in
we might feel great for a while,
but then it all goes wrong. What
things do you find tempting?

**Use a really easy code based on the
alphabet backwards! So 1 = Z, 2 = Y,
and so on until A = 26! Here's one to
try out.**

8 4 22 22 7 8

**Now write in number code things
that you find tempting**

Noah
A boat in the desert

BACKGROUND BIT

Place	Near the Garden of Eden in the desert
When	Some people think around 2,500 years before Jesus, others think a lot longer ago than that!
Job	Farmer, boat builder
Key bit	"Noah did everything the Lord told him to do." *Genesis 6:22*
Other guys	Sons called Ham, Shem and Japheth

If you were told to do the

total complete nuttiest opposite

to what makes sense, would you do it?

☐   ☐
YES   NO

Draw a line between one side and the things that go with them on the other:

Sky	Moon
Sea	School bag
Head	Road
Coffee	Boat
Foot	Chips
Game controller	Shoe
Books	Mug/cup
Neck	Hat
Fish	Game console
Car	Tie

Noah was a good man and obeyed God, but he and his family were pretty rare. Most people were living lives that were full of selfishness, greed, lies and hatred. God loved the world he'd created, but now people were making it really bad, so drastic measures were needed. God saw Noah and decided he was the one good guy who he should save. He saw the animals and birds he had made and decided that they'd done nothing wrong, and so many of them should be saved too. As for the rest of the humans – well, they had had their chance...

God told Noah to build a boat and gave really detailed instructions about how to build it. God told Noah the measurements, the type of wood... in fact, a whole construction manual! Day in and day out the boat got bigger, and the other people laughed, jeered and made jokes. Why? Well now, let's be clear on this – Noah and his wife and sons and their families lived in the desert. There wasn't much water about, and certainly the occasional puddles and wells weren't enough to float their boat! In fact, to be honest their boat was massive! In the end it was the length of about two football pitches.

Circle the things Noah needed to build his boat, and cross those things that wouldn't have been much help...

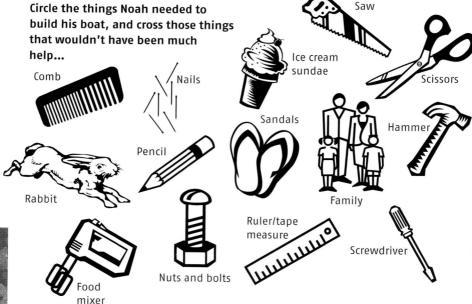

Saw

Ice cream sundae

Scissors

Comb

Nails

Sandals

Hammer

Pencil

Rabbit

Family

Ruler/tape measure

Screwdriver

Food mixer

Nuts and bolts

Paul Dixon flickr.com/people/yeti

What happened next?

- ◉ Noah had seven days to collect two of each animal and put them on the boat.
- ◉ Noah, his family and the animals were safe in the boat when it started to rain – it rained for 40 days.
- ◉ It took several months for the water to go down enough for the boat to rest on land.
- ◉ God promised Noah never to destroy the earth with a flood again.
- ◉ God put the sign of this in the sky.

What do you know about rainbows? They're an amazing sight, and it's easy to make your own small rainbow on a sunny day!

First Pour some clean water in a shallow bowl or deep plate.

Next Put a small mirror at an angle in the bowl.

Next Place the bowl near a window and stand the mirror so that sunlight hits it.

And... The light should bounce off the water and show a rainbow on the wall.

How much hero?

Length of life

950 years (...that's old!)   **100%**

Family

Wife and sons, dad Lamech   **80%**

Amazing moments

The flood and the rainbow   **90%**

Doing God's stuff

Built a boat despite what others said   **93%**

Generosity

Protected the animals and his family   **80%**

Strength

One of the few to keep in with God   **91%**

TOTAL HERO RATING   89%

Noah had to listen to God, and do a really weird thing. A boat and the desert didn't go together, but he stuck by what God had told him, and was safe. God sometimes expects us to do things that seem daft or foolish to others, but God really does know best. Noah was no fool... he was a hero!

Sometimes people think that Christians do strange and foolish things! We try to tell the truth instead of lying, and we aim to be kind and generous instead of selfish! But it takes a real hero to do the foolish things that God says are the right things to do. Are you up to it?

A quick look at
Abraham

Who was he?
Abraham was one of the first great leaders in the Bible, and is a really important Bible hero. A lot of what happened in the Bible was a result of Abraham obeying God, and going where God called him.

What did he do?
Abraham left all that was cosy, and set out to follow God and go where God led him. His faith in God was tested, but he always came out on top.

What did God do?
On one occasion God tested Abraham's faith by asking him to give up his most precious thing – his young son Isaac – to God.

What would you do?
You're old and you've waited to have a child for a really long time. Then God asks you to give up your son. Would you...

- ☐ Go ahead and follow God's plan.
- ☐ Refuse to do what God has asked you to do.
- ☐ Argue with God, and try to change his mind.
- ☐ The good news is that this was only a test, and God didn't take Isaac from Abraham.

How much hero?

Look up the Bible passages about Abraham below and decide on the hero rating for each.

Length of life
Genesis 25:7–8 ☐ %

Family
Genesis 11:29; 16:1–4,16; 21:2,3; 25:1,2 ☐ %

Amazing moments
Genesis 22 ☐ %

Doing God's stuff
Genesis 12:4–5 ☐ %

Generosity
Genesis 13:8–9 ☐ %

Strength
Genesis 18:16–33 ☐ %

TOTAL HERO RATING ☐ %

Why a hero?
Abraham started the whole of the Jewish nation, and sets everyone an example of how to trust God in the really tough times. He's got to be a hero!

Jacob
Selfish, godly and great

BACKGROUND BIT	
Place	Canaan
When	About 2,000 years before Jesus came along
Job	Farmer, animal-breeder
Key bit	"My grandfather Abraham and my father Isaac worshipped the Lord God. He has been with me all my life..." *Genesis 48:15*
Other guys	Dad Isaac, brother Esau, loads of famous sons

I wonder how many times you have said or thought, "It's not fair", and wanted to do something about it.

What's not fair in your life right now?

....

....

....

....

....

....

....

....

....

Sometimes things aren't fair at school! Do you think that it's fair that you have to go outside while the staff stay in and relax? Do you think it is fair that they get paid to come to school, but you have to do it for free? Sometimes life just doesn't seem fair!

Jacob made many people scream after him, "It's not fair". He was selfish, even as a teenager! His brother Esau was the eldest, and his dad's favourite. Esau did all the things his dad Isaac liked – he was a good hunter, loved being outdoors, had a great beard and was well-hairy! Jacob liked being around the home, was quiet and smooth-skinned, and his mum liked him best. Back then it was the tradition for the dad to bless his eldest son, and this meant a lot. Jacob's dad was old and blind, and so Jacob's mum suggested that Jacob should pretend to be Esau and steal his dad's blessing. So he put some fur over his arm, tried to imitate his brother's voice, and went to see his old dad, who was deceived by Jacob's lies and selfishness. He blessed him, and Esau was very angry... it wasn't fair!

Jacob finally left home with his father's blessing but little else, and headed out into the desert to find somewhere to work and to start his own family. One night he had a weird dream about a stairway to heaven, and then God spoke to him. He made an amazing promise to him.

Find out what it was by filling in the missing vowels to this staircase of words.

codebreaker

◉	⊜	⊙	◍	✦
a	e	i	o	u

th⊜ sp⊜cks ◍f d◉st.

◉s n⊙m⊜r◍⊙s ◉s

◍nd w◍ll b⊜c◉m⊜

⊙n ◍ll d⊙r⊜ct⊙◍ns

th⊜ ⊜◍rth

w◍ll spr⊜◍d ◍v⊜r

Y◍⊙r d⊜sc⊜nd⊙nts

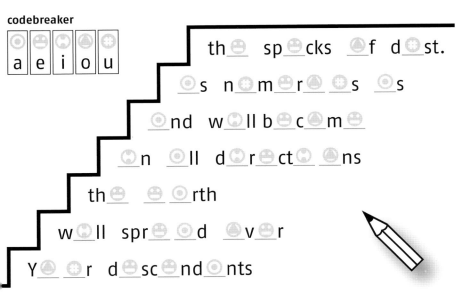

What happened next?

- Jacob was a successful farmer.
- Jacob married Leah and Rachel. (Having more than one wife was allowed back then!)
- Jacob offered Esau loads of gifts as his way of saying a big "sorry".
- Jacob had 12 sons, who became the leaders of the twelve tribes of Israel.
- His favourite son was Joseph (see the next Bible hero).
- Jacob lost most of his wealth when there was a famine in his country.

What do you think Esau said when Jacob offered him loads of gifts?

I'm so angry I could kill you

Oh, the cheat has come to see me at last!

Keep what you have, I don't need it.

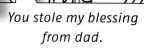

I'm OK – things have worked out well.

Can you add anything you may have said if you were Esau?

....

....

....

....

....

You stole my blessing from dad.

Are you still a selfish guy?

Jacob was worried that Esau would attack him and take all that he had, but instead Esau was forgiving... he was a hero too!

Jacob is a hero despite his selfish beginning and the times he went wrong during his life. He grew to know that God had been really generous and kind, and trusted God more and more the older he got. His name lives on as the big daddy – the father of many nations.

Mark these selfish acts one to five with five being the most selfish:

☐ You have two sweets left, and your friend wants one...but you eat them both.

☐ An old lady wants help crossing the road, but you leave her 'cus you want to go to play football.

☐ You're given money for a charity event at school, but you keep it and spend it at the shop on the way home.

☐ Your friend loses their homework, but you don't help them do it again.

☐ Your mum asks you to help set the table but you refuse because you want to watch the TV.

How much hero?

Length of life
147 **85%**

Family
12 famous sons, dad Isaac, bro Esau **90%**

Amazing moments
Cheating his brother, dream from God **80%**

Doing God's stuff
Relied on God, led a great family **85%**

Generosity
Became less selfish, said sorry to Esau **83%**

Strength
Bad start, but came to rely on God **72%**

TOTAL HERO RATING **82.5%**

Jacob's life is told in Genesis 25–50. There's a lot of it!

Wrestling with God

A man came and fought with Jacob until just before daybreak. When the man saw that he could not win, he struck Jacob on the hip and threw it out of joint. They kept on wrestling until the man said, "Let go of me! It's almost daylight."

"You can't go until you bless me," Jacob replied.

Then the man asked, "What is your name?"

"Jacob," he answered.

The man said, "Your name will no longer be Jacob. You have wrestled with God and with men, and you have won. That's why your name will be Israel." Jacob said, "Now tell me your name."

"Don't you know who I am?" he asked. And he blessed Jacob.

Jacob said, "I have seen God face to face, and I am still alive." So he named the place Peniel. The sun was coming up as Jacob was leaving Peniel. He was limping because he had been struck on the hip, and the muscle on his hip joint had been injured. That's why even today the people of Israel don't eat the hip muscle of any animal. Genesis 32:24–32

Jacob was part of an amazing experience – he wrestled with God and came out alive...but a little bit injured! When we pray God wants us to wrestle with the things that are really bothering us, deep down as well as on the surface.

Think about the things that really get to you, the tough decisions you need to make, and the things about the world or the church that you think are really bad and wrong. Write a few words about them onto Jacob.

Now pray, and tell God how you REALLY feel. If you can, go outside to a park or field and shout some of the things! The more we tell God what's really going on with us and 'wrestle' with those things, the more God hears us and helps us.

A quick look at
Joseph

Who was he?
Joseph was one of the 12 sons of Jacob, and his favourite. He was given a wonderful coat by his dad.

What did he do?
Joe had dreams that his brothers would bow to him. They got jealous and sold him to be a slave. He was a good slave in Egypt but got blamed for something he'd not done, ended up in prison, and got out by explaining the Pharaoh's dreams. In the end he was rich and powerful, and his brothers came from their land to beg him for help.

What did God do?
God really looked after Joseph, even in the tough times. He gave him some chances, and the gift of explaining dreams which helped him loads!

What would you do?
You've been thrown into jail for something you've not done, and there seems to be no way out. Would you...

☐ Tell God you've given up and he's been no help at all

☐ Try to escape in any way you can

☐ Trust God to give you a chance and help you again

How much hero?

Look up the Bible passages about Joseph below and decide on the hero rating for each.

Length of life Genesis 50:22	☐	%
Family Genesis 48:1	☐	%
Amazing moments Genesis 45	☐	%
Doing God's stuff Genesis 41	☐	%
Generosity Genesis 45:4–8	☐	%
Strength Genesis 39:19–23	☐	%

TOTAL HERO RATING ☐ %

Why a hero?
Joseph went through some amazing and scary times and was rejected by his own brothers. Despite all that he still stuck with God, and in the end forgave his brothers for their nasty behaviour and lies.

BIBLE HEROES

21

How much hero?

Look up the Bible passages about Moses below and decide on the hero rating for each.

Length of life
Deuteronomy 34:7 [ ] %

Family
Exodus 2:4; 18:2–4 [ ] %

Amazing moments
Exodus 14 [ ] %

Doing God's stuff
Deuteronomy 34:10–12 [ ] %

Generosity
Exodus 2:15–20 [ ] %

Strength
Exodus 17:1–7 [ ] %

TOTAL HERO RATING [ ] %

Why a hero?
Moses was a brilliant leader despite his mistakes when younger. God helped him and changed him.

A quick look at
Moses

Who was he?
Moses was the leader God chose to take his people from being slaves in Egypt to the edge of a great new land.

What did he do?
Moses was hidden as a baby, put in a basket in a river, and adopted by a princess. He killed someone and then hid as a shepherd for many years before God spoke to him and told him to lead the people. Moses challenged the leader of Egypt known as Pharaoh, and God allowed bad things to happen until the people were free. Moses led the people from Egypt, took them through a dry path in the middle of a sea, and led them through a wilderness for many years.

What did God do?
God called, helped and led Moses, and even trusted him to receive God's rules which were known as the Ten Commandments.

What would you do?
You're on the edge of the sea with thousands of people who trust you, no boats, and an army chasing after you. Would you....

[ ] Pray really, really hard until God tells you what to do

[ ] Tell the people to learn to swim fast!

[ ] Turn around and surrender to the enemy

Praying for others

Moses returned to the LORD and said, "The people have committed a terrible sin. They have made a gold idol to be their god. But I beg you to forgive them. If you don't, please wipe my name out of your book." Exodus 32:31–32

Moses was a really cool guy! After all he had done and been through, he came back down the mountain after talking with God to find that the people had failed him and failed God again. They had made a statue out of gold and were worshipping it. He could have walked away from them, shouted at them, or given up on them. He could have asked God to punish them strongly or turn away from them. But instead of giving up on them, he prayed hard to God that he would forgive them. Moses hated what they had done, but loved them anyway!

Moses showed us the way, as he prayed that God would forgive those people. Follow that great example – think of these people, write their names or draw their faces, and pray for them. We might not see the results of these prayers, but God always listens!

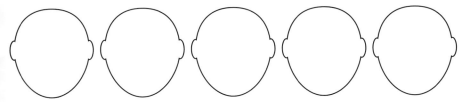

① Who has upset you by what they have done?

① Who makes you really cross?

① Who seems to get away with bad things all the time?

Joshua
Learned and led

Place	Egypt, the wilderness, the Promised Land
When	1,500 years before Jesus, or 3,500 years before now!
Job	Priest, warrior, leader
Key bit	"I've commanded you to be strong and brave. Don't ever be afraid or discouraged!" *Joshua 1:9*
Other guys	Moses, Aaron

Many of us have people we look up to, learn from, and want to be like. They could be friends or family, heroes on TV or celebs. When we have the opportunity to be able to learn from someone who wants to help us then we should take the chance.

Who do you want to be like?
Draw or paste a photo in the picture frame.

Joshua had been a slave in Egypt, and was one of those who escaped slavery with Moses. He had watched when Moses had prayed to God and an amazing path had appeared through the sea so he and the people could escape. He had stood to one side as Moses prayed and God provided food for the people to eat out in the wild, rough and lonely desert. And Moses knew that Joshua was there, and knew that he was gonna be good!

God's people took 40 years to find their way to the land that God had promised them, and on the way there were battles to be had. Moses appointed the young Josh to be the leader of the army, and told him what to do. And as Moses stood and held out his hand as a sign of God's help, the Amalekites were completely smashed by Joshua. This was the start of a brave and often very bloody fighting career for the young leader.

Joshua learned from Moses, and knew that with God on his side he couldn't go too far wrong. Many years later, after Moses had died, God gave this command to Joshua:

I've commanded you to be strong and brave. Don't ever be afraid or discouraged!

What would you say if you'd been Joshua?

I don't want to fight battles!

Can I have lots of money to do this?

I'm not brave enough!

OK, I believe and trust you, God.

Are you sure you will be with me?

What happened next?

- Josh led the people across the River Jordan – he asked God for help, the water stopped flowing, and a shallow path was there!
- Josh led the people to set up stones to remind them of God's goodness.
- Josh led the people through many battles including one in Jericho.

The people of Jericho would have always been trouble, so Josh's army were told to go into the city and kill every person except a few who God wanted saving. However, Jericho was a large town surrounded by a strong, high wall. How would they achieve their goal? Here's how it happened...

- Josh got his instructions while praying to God
- The army marched around the outside of the city wall once a day for six days
  - On day seven they marched around it seven times, shouted loud, and...
    - The whole city collapsed

Here's a maze of walls and rubble after the city collapsed. Try to find your way to the centre through the maze, like Joshua's army did.

So is Josh a hero? He was brill at fighting battles, and a great example to all the other people, but most of all he copied Moses, and lived his life listening to God as Moses had shown him. Heroes do that!

If you're gonna be a hero for God, then it's great if there's someone that you can look up to. Is there anyone you know who is a hero for God...who does great things, stands up for Jesus, or sets a cool example? If there is, that's the person to be like! Write their name here:

....

....

....

How much hero?

Length of life
110 great years   **95%**

Family
Dad was called Nun   **75%**

Amazing moments
Loads of battles and fighting   **90%**

Doing God's stuff
Led the people and obeyed God   **90%**

Generosity
A fair and respected leader   **85%**

Strength
Really great warrior, never gave up   **89%**

TOTAL HERO RATING   87.3%

The first few books of the Old Testament at the start of the Bible have lots of Josh. You can find him in Exodus, Numbers, Deuteronomy, Joshua and Judges.

Gideon

A little guy gets big!

BACKGROUND BIT

Place	Ophrah and Jezreel, nation of Israel
When	1,200 years before Jesus was born
Job	Farmer, fighter, judge
Key bit	"Then the Lord himself said, 'Gideon, you will be strong, because I am giving you the power to rescue Israel from the Midianites'" *Judges 6:14*
Other guys	Angel, small army, massive family!

Which of these things would you love to do, and which would you hate doing?

CLEARING OUT A PIG-STY

parachute JUMPING

Jet skiing

Singing a solo in public

Leading an army in a vital battle

Climbing a mountain

Reading a poem **out loud** in school

Clearing out your bedroom

Gidi was a little guy, and he knew it. Life was tough as a poor farmer, and Gidi tried to keep his head down and make enough bread to survive. Gidi was the youngest and weakest of his family, and his family were the poorest and weakest of the whole clan...and tribe...and nation! Poor Gidi really didn't have much going for him!

Times were also tough for the whole nation of Israel, because they'd decided they knew better than God, and so their enemies the Midis from nearby Midian were slowly taking over. As the Midis got closer Gidi decided to hide away and grind some wheat...like little guys do!

Gidi was a little startled when an angel came to him and said:

Gidi, God says you've got to go and rescue all your people from the Midis

Me? You're havin' a laugh! I'm the weakest of the weak!

Gideon

God told Gidi that he could do it with his help, and Gidi started to get the people ready and told them not to worship silly statues! But even then Gidi still wasn't sure, so he tested God. He asked God to make the ground dry overnight, and a fleecy rug wet, which God did. He then asked God to do it the other way round, with the ground being wet and the fleece dry... which God did. Gidi was learning, but slowly!

What happened next?

- God didn't want a huge army to fight the Midis, because then the people would forget that he is all-powerful and would continue to ignore him.
- So Gidi had to trust God as his army got smaller... and smaller... and smaller!
- Gidi was left with just 300 men who surrounded the Midi army camp with jars, torch flames and trumpets.
- At Gidi's signal they made as much noise as possible, This confused the Midis who ran away, tripped over and fought each other... they were defeated big-time.
- Gidi looked after the nation for 40 years and there was peace instead of battles.

- Gidi became a judge. He did all that God said and treated the people well.
- But he didn't encourage his family to follow God, and the whole nation soon forgot to trust God after he died.

How do you think Gidi was remembered? Write your ideas on his gravestone.

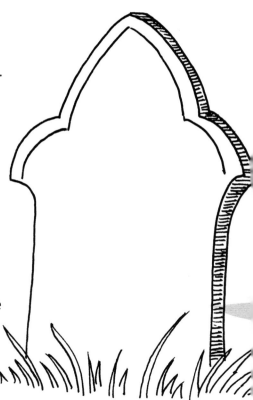

A little man thinking that he was pretty useless becomes a great leader and wins an amazing battle with only a few on his side. There's no doubt that Gidi was a hero.

We can all feel little sometimes, even if we're tall! We can think that we don't matter, or that we are too unimportant to be a hero.

Measure yourself – how tall are you? Write it in here:

....

....

God can use you if you're tall or small...you can be a Gidi-like hero!

How much hero?

Length of life
The Bible says he was 'a ripe old age'! **80%**

Family
70 sons and many wives! **90%**

Amazing moments
The battle against the Midis **90%**

Doing God's stuff
Learned to trust God, but didn't
get his family to! **75%**

Generosity
A fair judge and a cool leader **80%**

Strength
Grew stronger and braver **75%**

TOTAL HERO RATING	81.6%

Gidi's full story is in Judges 6–8, in the Old Testament of the Bible. It's a bit gory, with lots of soldiers ending up dead!

Samuel

Listening boy, leading man

Place	Ephraim, Shiloh
When	3,000 years in the past
Job	Priest, prophet, leader
Key bit	"As Samuel grew up, the Lord helped him and made everything Samuel said come true." *1 Samuel 3:19*
Other guys	Eli, Hannah, Kings Saul and David

What can you hear right now, as you read this?

music

hoover

birds

silence

singing

It's so important to listen, even if what we have to listen to is boring and unimportant, 'cos you never know when something stunning is going to be said!

Hannah was a lady who had prayed and prayed to God for years, but must have thought that God wasn't listening to her prayers. She kept asking God to allow her and her husband to have a child, but as she got older the more impossible it seemed to be. In desperation one day she prayed that, if she had a son, she would give him to God to work in the temple with the priest Eli. God heard, she had a son, and when he was just a few years old she kept her promise. She took her only son back to the temple and handed him over to the care of Eli the priest so he could learn to work for God.

What jobs do you think young Samuel had to do for the old priest Eli? Tick which of these you think are most likely:

Cleaning

Cleaning his car

Working on computer

Keeping Eli company

Setting up for worship

Tidying up

Lighting candles

Praying

What happened next?

- Eli's grown-up sons didn't listen to God, ignored their father and did heaps of bad things.
- God chose to speak to Samuel about it – he called his name three times in the night.
- At first Samuel thought it was Eli and ran to him, but the third time, Eli realised it was God and told Samuel to reply, 'Speak, I am listening.'
- When God spoke again, Sam said, 'Speak, I am listening' and God told him that he would punish Eli's sons.
- Sam told Eli the bad news and he accepted that God is the boss.
- Sam grew, and listened to God more and more.
- By the time he was a man he was a priest, and a special messenger of God.
- He became ruler of Israel, and did tons of stuff that was good and not a lot that wasn't!
- But sadly, a bit like his old friend Eli, he wasn't able to get his sons to love God like he did.

Which of these do you think best fits what Sam must have been thinking after hearing the message from God about Eli's sons?

I don't want to tell him this, but I know I must

I think I'll forget what God told me

Wow, what a message! I can't wait to blab to Eli

It must all have been a bad dream

Life was busy for Samuel, even as a young boy working in that temple. But he still knew to stop and listen, to hear what God had to say, and to pass God's message on. Sam was a total hero boy and a complete hero man!

How good are you at listening? Here's a list of people you could ask, and write in what they say! Ask them: "Am I good at listening?"

Mum, dad or other
adult at home

....

....

Friend

....

....

Brother/sister

....

....

Teacher

....

....

How much hero?

Length of life
God's messenger all his long life   **80%**

Family
Mother: Hannah
Children: Joel and Abijah   **85%**

Amazing moments
Hearing God speak, anointing
David as king   **80%**

Doing God's stuff
Messenger, prophet and judge   **85%**

Generosity
Worked for God and for everyone   **95%**

Strength
Spoke out, even though it was tough   **92%**

TOTAL HERO RATING   86.1%

The first time God spoke to Samuel is in 1 Samuel chapter 3. The rest of his long life is through 1 Samuel up to chapter 28.

Listening to God

The LORD then stood beside Samuel and called out as he had done before, "Samuel! Samuel!"
"I'm listening," Samuel answered. "What do you want me to do?" 1 Samuel 3:10

What do you do when you pray? There are loads of ways to pray, and God speaks to us in many ways too. When we stop and listen to God he lets us know by changing the way we feel, like making us feel calm and peaceful inside. Sometimes we will really know the words God is saying to us... they come into our minds. We may find ourselves looking and finding things in the Bible that we weren't expecting to, or we might just know, deep inside, what God wants us to do.

Try to spend some time being a bit like Samuel. Here's how:

1. Find somewhere quiet to sit and relax.
2. Spend a bit of time clearing your mind of other things, concentrating on God.
3. Think or say out loud "Speak, Lord, I'm listening".
4. Ask God to show you that he is there.
5. Chill out and allow God to speak in any of the ways he does!
6. Be ready to feel calmed and happy, to have new ideas, and to know deep inside what God is saying just to you.

When you feel God is telling you to do something it's good to check it out with someone else who is in touch with God, and get their wise advice too.

David
The faulty king of all heroes

BACKGROUND BIT

Place	Bethlehem and Jerusalem
When	1,000 years before God sent Jesus to the earth
Job	Shepherd, poet, musician, king, warrior
Key bit	"At that moment the Spirit of the LORD took control of David and stayed with him from then on." *1 Samuel 16:13*
Other guys	King Saul, Jonathan, Samuel

We don't really have kings like they had kings way back in the Bible. Then kings had all power and all authority... unless they got in the way of God, of course!

If you were a super-powerful king what would:

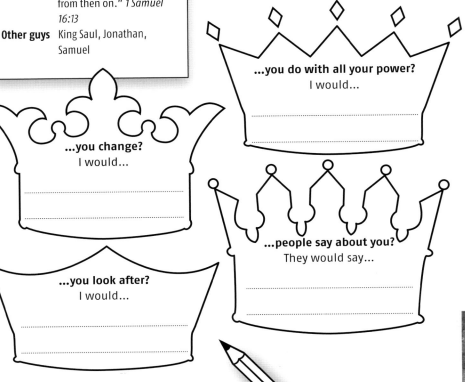

...you do with all your power?
I would...

...you change?
I would...

...people say about you?
They would say...

...you look after?
I would...

David was a great king and for much of his life he was helped by his faith and trust in God. There's a lot in his life story, so we're going to look at just a few key moments.

David was just a boy when God chose him to be a future king, but at that point he just worked for his dad in the fields caring for their flocks of sheep. He was good at it, and brave enough to protect the sheep from wild animals. But the surprise for the whole country came when David said he was brave enough to fight a giant! The army was really scared of the giant Goliath, who was huge, and so they didn't think much of this little lad offering to take him on...

What do you think they said?

David's brothers and dad thought he was an idiot!

What do you think they said?

But David somehow knew that God was on his side, even though Goliath had a good giggle at him.

What do you think Goliath said?

David picked up a stone and, using a little sling, chucked it at Goliath. It hit him right in the middle of his head, and killed him in a second. The ground shook as he fell to the floor, and for the first of many times David was proclaimed a hero!

What happened next?

◉ David plays the harp for King Saul.

◉ David becomes great friends with the king's son, Jonathan.

◉ King Saul gets jealous of David, and tries to kill him.

◉ David takes over as king and leads the army in many battles.

◉ David arranges for Bathsheba's husband to be killed so that he can marry Bathsheba.

◉ David marries Bathsheba.

◉ Nathan helps David to see his mistake.

◉ David's son dies.

◉ David writes loads of poems and songs.

David won lots and lots of battles. Here are some of the nations and lands he defeated.

SCOREBOARD			
David	1	0	Geshurites
David	4	1	Girzites
David	3	0	Amelekites
David	2	1	Ish's* army
David	3	0	Jerusalem
David	2	1	Philistines
David	3	1	Damascus
David	4	0	Zoba
David	3	0	Edomites

*Ishbosheth *see 2 Samuel 2:8–17*

BIBLE HEROES

How much hero?

Length of life
Was king for 40 years, and
called 'very old'   **80%**

Family
Loads of brothers, wives,
and children!   **80%**

Amazing moments
Killing Goliath, becoming king   **90%**

Doing God's stuff
Obeyed God and did a good
job as boss   **80%**

Generosity
Kind to his friends...
tough on his enemies   **80%**

Strength
Gave in to temptation a bit too often! **60%**

TOTAL HERO RATING   78.3%

David's name is mentioned all through
the Bible. The main bits of his story are
in 1 and 2 Samuel, and his songs and
poems are in Psalms.

David was the greatest ever King of Israel, and is remembered for his many children, his brill leadership, and his stunning battle victories. He was no goody-goody, but a guy like us who God really loved and cared about, but who got it wrong. Even as one of the most powerful kings ever in all history, David learned to ask for God to forgive him, and tried hard to change how he lived. A hero with failings – just like us!

What things do you do that aren't quite what you should? Write these here in your own code or draw symbols in the boxes below:

Saying sorry

You are kind, God! Please have pity on me.
  You are always merciful!
    Please wipe away my sins.
Wash me clean from all of my sin and guilt.
I know about my sins,
  and I cannot forget my terrible guilt.
You are really the one I have sinned against;
  I have disobeyed you and have done wrong.
So it is right and fair for you
  to correct and punish me.

I have sinned and done wrong since the day I
  was born.
But you want complete honesty,
  so teach me true wisdom.
Wash me with hyssop
  until I am clean and whiter than snow.
Let me be happy and joyful!
  You crushed my bones, now let them
    celebrate.
Turn your eyes from my sin and cover my guilt.
Create pure thoughts in me
  and make me faithful again.

Psalm 51:1–10

David was a great hero...and went really, really wrong too! Heroes know when they do the wrong things, and know what to do about it! David knew that the best thing to do was to say sorry to God. God knows whether we mean our "sorry" or not, and promises to completely, totally forgive anyone who says sorry and really means it!

Use two different colours of highlighter pen. Highlight first the things David says he did wrong, and spend a bit of time thinking about those things and whether you have gone wrong like that too.

Now use the other pen to highlight the way David wants to be, and what he is asking God to do with and for him. Say some of those things out loud for yourself, asking God those things too.

Joash
Young king, smooth operator!

Place	Jerusalem and land of Judah
When	3,000 years ago
Job	King
Key bit	"...Joash obeyed the Lord." *2 Kings 12:2*
Other guys	Jehoida, Zechariah

What do you think is important to most boys aged 7?

You may never have heard of Joash – he's not a very well-known guy in the Bible. But Joash was both a hero and a disaster during his life.

When Joash was born, things were pretty tough, and the violent and nasty Queen Athaliah was on the throne. She gave orders that all the children of the previous king should be killed, including the tiny baby Joash. But the wife of a priest, one of God's good guys called Jehoida, saw what was happening and was really bright! She got hold of Joash and hid him in a secret room in the temple, with someone to look after him, for six years until he was seven. Then things really started to take off...

Queen Athaliah was really hated, and only a few years into her reign she was killed. Then the son of the previous king was the only one left to take over, and that was young Joash. So at the age of seven he was able to come out of hiding and take over as the king. Wow... not a bad deal!

Now the great thing about King Joash, being so young, was that he was willing to listen and be guided by others. He didn't think he knew it all, but instead trusted the priest Jehoida to help him, and things went from good to even better!

There are plenty of people who may offer us advice, but it's not always the best thing to listen to them, or to do what they say!

Who are the people you listen to? Any of these? Any others?

Others:

- [ ] Mum
- [ ] Dad
- [ ] Uncle
- [ ] Brother or sister
- [ ] Teacher
- [ ] Friends
- [ ] Pop stars/celebs

What happened next?

- Joash listened to Jehoiada, and took the good advice he was offered.
- He was a really good king, and followed all the stuff that God wanted really carefully.
- Joash organised the rebuilding of the temple.
- However, when Jehoiada died, our hero turned to zero!
- Others nagged at King Joash to change things. He was now older and thought he should make his own mind up rather than follow wise advice.
- Within a few years the temple was left empty and the people were praying and singing songs to any old statues and stuff they could find.

What do you think happened after that? Have a go at putting these in order:

__ __ __ __ __ __

Answer on page 95.

A	Joash and his army lost the battle.
B	God wasn't too pleased and sent Zechariah, Jehoiada's son, to tell the people to turn back to him.
C	Joash was badly injured, and then two of his own leaders finished him off.
D	The people continued to worship silly idols.
E	Zechariah was murdered, and King Joash arranged it.
F	The Syrians attacked Judah and a big battle began.

Oh dear – it all went really pear-shaped! King Joash had been a great leader when he was young. He learned from God and did the right thing, listening to those who could give good advice. As he got older he thought he knew it all, and it turned out that he didn't!

Young people often know the right thing to do, so remember that when you have your own opinions and feel strongly about what's right.

How much hero?

Length of life
Oldish, but murder got in the way!   **70%**

Family
Father King Amaziah, son Jotham   **80%**

Amazing moments
King aged 7, rebuilt the temple   **72%**

Doing God's stuff
Listening to Jehoiada's wisdom   **60%**

Generosity
Great...until he got older!   **70%**

Strength
Listening to wisdom for a while   **65%**

TOTAL HERO RATING   69.5%

Joash as a boy and as a man are written about in 2 Chronicles 24 and 2 Kings 11:1 – 14:23

How much hero?

Look up the Bible passages about Jonah below and decide on the hero rating for each.

Length of life
Unknown
[ ] %

Family
Jonah 1:1
[ ] %

Amazing moments
Jonah 1:17
[ ] %

Doing God's stuff
Jonah 3:3
[ ] %

Generosity
Jonah 4:10–11
[ ] %

Strength
Jonah 3:3–4
[ ] %

TOTAL HERO RATING [ ] %

A quick look at
Jonah

Who was he?
Jonah was a prophet that God wanted to go to the town of Ninevah to tell them off!

What did he do?
Jonah wasn't keen on being God's messenger to a really bad town, so he jumped on a boat and tried to escape God. There was a huge storm, the boat crew threw Jonah into the rough sea, and he ended up inside a huge, stinky and slimy fish!

What did God do?
God always forgives, and only stupid people ignore that! Jonah prayed, God heard, and before long the fish sicked him up onto some land.

What would you do?
You've had a bit of a scary adventure, but still God is telling you to go to a nasty place and give them tough news. Would you...

[ ] Tell God there's no deal, and you just want to go home

[ ] Do as God told you to and see what happens

[ ] Promise to go, but after you're free from the fish, run away again!

Why a hero?
OK, so Jonah isn't the best example of the perfect guy, but he was real and had real doubts and fears that we all have. In the end he did what God called him to do...and he got a book in the Bible all about it!

From inside the fish, Jonah prayed to the LORD his God:

When I was in trouble, LORD,
I prayed to you,
    and you listened to me.
From deep in the world
    of the dead,
I begged for your help,
    and you answered my prayer.

You threw me down
    to the bottom of the sea.
The water was churning
    all around;
I was completely covered
    by your mighty waves.
I thought I was swept away
    from your sight,
never again to see
    your holy temple.

I was almost drowned
by the swirling waters
    that surrounded me.

Jonah 2:1–5

God wants his heroes to be honest with him! We can tell God anything, and he really listens and cares. Write some things in the boxes, and remember to be completely, massively honest!

Remember — Jonah prayed honestly when he was in a mess, and we can too.

When in trouble

God, I like

but I don't like

I get really cross about

and I don't think it's fair that

I find it really, really tough when

Isaiah
Master of the messages!

BACKGROUND BIT

Place	Jerusalem
When	700 years before Jesus
Job	Messenger from God
Key bit	"I'll go," I answered. "Send me!" *Isaiah 6:8*
Other guys	Kings, including Hezekiah

Have a look at a newspaper or the news on the Internet. Count up how many "good news" stories there are, and how many "bad news".

Bad news isn't nice to hear. Most of us like to be able to have good news, to say good news, and to make others happy. But if your job is to be a messenger of God then sometimes hard things have to be said, even if those who hear don't like the message!

Bad News total	
Good News total	

Isaiah grew up in a difficult time for God's people. The nation of Judah seemed to go from one great king to the next rubbish one, and very often they took no notice of God. So God needed prophets – messengers who would speak out to the leaders and the kings, to challenge them, and to tell them off in God's name! This was a risky job, and could easily have ended in being killed.

Isaiah was having a dream when God clearly spoke to him directly. This made Isaiah pretty scared, as any of us would be. Isaiah knew that he was in the presence of God, and immediately told God just how bad he was. But God wasn't interested in all that – he was looking for a messenger. Isaiah didn't even need to think about it – he knew God was calling him, and he knew he had to do it!

What would your response be if God called you to...

	YES	NO	MAYBE
Tell people nice things	☐	☐	☐
Do what he asked you to	☐	☐	☐
Give people bad news	☐	☐	☐
Take his messages across the world	☐	☐	☐

Secret recipe for curing boils

Ingredients
- 3 good-sized figs
- boiling water

What to do
Add boiling water to the figs and mash to make a paste. Apply to infected boil on skin.

What happened next?

◉ Isaiah continued to take messages from God to all the people of the nation and to the king.

◉ Most of the messages were warnings to turn from doing bad to good. People didn't always want to listen!

◉ Isaiah helped King Hezekiah who was really frightened of the people in the next country, Assyria. The king sent messengers, and God told Isaiah what to say.

◉ King Hezekiah became very ill. God told Isaiah to put a paste of figs on the infected boil on the king's skin. Three days after Isaiah followed these instructions, the king was healed.

◉ That king went on to live for another 15 years, and with Isaiah's help kept the people on track.

◉ Isaiah was also a great writer, and wrote down what God told him.

◉ He wrote about the coming of Jesus – 700 years later it all came true!

Isaiah was spot on about Jesus, even though he lived 700 years before Jesus was born. Match them up by joining them with different colours:

He was wounded and crushed for our sins. *Isaiah 53:5*

None of the important people knew what to do with Jesus, so they asked the people, who shouted "Crucify him!"

Mary gave birth to Jesus, and Emmanuel means "God with us".

He was condemned to death without a fair trial. *Isaiah 53:8*

Jesus was arrested and then beaten and abused.

A young woman is pregnant, she will have a son and name him Emmanuel. *Isaiah 7:14*

He was painfully abused, but did not complain. *Isaiah 53:7*

Jesus was wounded and then put on the cross.

Isaiah lived a life completely given over to God. He was brave enough to speak out to the leaders, and honest enough to know that he made mistakes like everyone else. Without him we would know a lot less about the coming of Jesus and a lot less about how to live right – he's a hero!

Isaiah travelled from place to place talking to people and explaining God's messages. On the previous page you will see Isaiah, ready to go! Add to the picture all the things he may have taken with him, for example:

- Cloak
- Walking stick
- Donkey
- Rolls of paper or parchment*
- Spare sandals
- Coins

*Parchment is an old form of paper. **Find out more about it, and write what you find out here:**

....

....

....

....

How much hero?

Length of life
Old – he outlived five kings!   **80%**

Family
Dad Amoz, two sons   **80%**

Amazing moments
Saying "yes" to God,
loads of messages   **90%**

Doing God's stuff
Listened carefully to God
and spoke out   **90%**

Generosity
Gave his life to be a prophet   **85%**

Strength
Stuck at it without fear   **85%**

TOTAL HERO RATING	85%

There's a bit about Isaiah's life in 2 Kings 19–21, and lots of his messages and prophecies in the book of Isaiah.

Daniel
Taking a dare seriously!

BACKGROUND BIT

Place	Babylon and Persia
When	600 years BC
Job	Servant to the king, leader, godly guy
Key bit	"My God knew that I was innocent, and he sent an angel to keep the lions from eating me." *Daniel 6:21*
Other guys	King Neb and King Darius, friends

We often talk about dares, but the dares we do aren't likely to affect our whole lives, put us at risk of death, or change history! This hero was a young guy who dared to be so different and so true to God that even the king took notice.

Have you ever dared someone else to do something? Did they do it? What happened? Fill in the chart.

What dare?	Who?	What happened?

Daniel had not had the best of starts! Sometime while he was growing up his country was smashed in a battle, and Daniel was taken away from home to live in Babylon. There he was chosen to train to be one of the really special servants of King Nebuchadnezzar (let's call him King Neb!). He'd got friends with him, and learned well.

Daniel's first dare was to refuse to eat the king's food! Now, just to remind you, this was a captive, given a great opportunity, but not really able to argue! Daniel dared to ask for vegetables instead of the king's dodgy nosh, and he was so fit and healthy on his veggie diet that it worked, and he was allowed to carry on. Dare one done!

We don't really know what food the King was serving, and what veg Daniel ate... but here's a guess! How many of these foods can you find here?

Grapes   Bread   Meat
Peas   Carrots   Honey
Fish   Apple   Bran
Avocado   Rice   Veal

C	L	R	I	C	E	H	B	C	M
A	V	O	C	A	D	O	P	A	J
P	E	C	B	R	A	N	J	R	S
P	A	G	R	A	P	E	S	R	A
L	L	B	E	L	E	Y	W	O	I
E	M	E	A	T	A	S	A	T	A
R	G	N	D	G	S	F	I	S	H
T	H	E	R	B	S	K	M	G	O

Daniel was really good at stuff, but he knew God had given him those abilities, and he never forgot to thank God for it. So a few years later, when King Neb had died and his son Darius had taken over, some jealous guys ganged up on Dan, and he dared yet again. Here's what happened...

1 Some jealous men persuaded the King to force people to worship him.

2 Daniel did not worship to the king – he dared to carry on praying to God.

3 The jealous cheats got the king to agree that people who didn't worship him would be fed to lions.

4 Daniel was found to be praying to God, not the king, but still dared to refuse, so he was put in a pit full of lions.

5 The lions left Daniel alone.... they didn't seem peckish!

6 King Darius was so pleased that he ordered people to worship God, and threw the cheating men to the lions, who by then had become very hungry!

Daniel went on to do loads and loads of great stuff for God, and was one of those amazing people who quietly dared to stick to what was right, whatever anyone else said. The dares Daniel did were not just a game – they were about life and death. Because he dared to stand up for truth others saw that God was really cool, and a whole nation changed the way it lived and worshipped. Some hero!

Life is full of tough choices, especially when you're in BIG trouble! Here's some to think about...what would you do?

1 You're on a boat on a river with crocodiles. Suddenly you're surrounded. Do you:
a) Shoot them with your water pistol.
b) Throw in your peanut butter sandwich to distract them and swim to shore.
c) Pray hard and act quick?

2 You face a tough punishment in a strict place because you're one of God's heroes. Do you:
a) Stick with God and trust him to help.
b) Cry, shout, scream, and promise to buy everyone an ice cream if they let you go.
c) Change all your beliefs and promise to give up on God?

How much hero?

Length of life
A long life of trusting God **80%**

Family
Probably separated from them when young **75%**

Amazing moments
Explaining dreams, surviving lions **90%**

Doing God's stuff
Dared to quietly do the right thing **90%**

Generosity
A great servant, a great leader... **90%**

Strength
Daring to face death for God **90%**

TOTAL HERO RATING **85.8%**

Daniel has a whole book in the Bible about his life, and it's a great story to read!

Prayer page
Praising God

"Our God, your name
will be praised
        for ever and for ever.
You are all-powerful,
        and you know everything.
You control human events –
you give rulers their power
        and take it away,
and you are the source
        of wisdom and knowledge.

" You explain deep mysteries,
because even the dark
        is light to you.
You are the God
who was worshipped
        by my ancestors.
Now I thank you and
        praise you
        for making me wise
and telling me the king's dream,
        together with its meaning."

Daniel 2:20–23

Churches often talk about praising God, and God wants us to praise him... but do we always know what it means? How do you feel if someone praises you? I guess you feel good, and have a warm, happy feeling inside! God has given us all so much good stuff, that it is right to praise him.

Have a look at Daniel's great prayer of praise. Pick out five of the phrases and descriptions of what God has done that you really like. Write each of those five into a balloon.

Now think about things God has done for you, and all that he has given you. Write five of those personal things into the other balloons. Once you've done all that, find a quiet place and say them out loud as your praise to God today!

Simeon
Waiting for a special child

Place	Jerusalem
When	2,000 years ago, just after Jesus was born
Job	Retired
Key bit	"With my own eyes I have seen what you have done to save your people." *Luke 2:30*
Other guys	Mary, Joseph, Jesus, Anna

What do you have to wait for? Any of these? Anything else?

☐ Mum or dad
☐ Favourite TV programme
☐ School to end
☐ Use the shower
☐ Best friend
☐ The bus
☐ Your turn to play
☐ Lunch

Others:

....

....

....

....

....

Jesus had been born some weeks before, and the family were by then in Jerusalem. His parents were careful to do the right thing and stick with God's law, so when the time came for Jesus to be taken to the temple Mary and Joseph got ready and headed there.

That same morning an old man called Simeon, who lived in Jerusalem, was guided by God to go to the temple. We don't know whether God spoke to him in a voice, or he just had a feeling inside that he had to go there, but Simeon was soon on his way. Simeon knew from the scriptures that God was going to send someone special to save the world, and he really felt that he wouldn't die until he saw him for himself.

By the time we know anything about Simeon he is an old man, and we don't know what work he did before he retired. But we do know some really great things about him:

So how would people describe you? Draw your face and note down what you think people would say.

Full of the Holy Spirit

Trusted God

Looked forward, not back

Guided by God

Knew God was at work

A really good man

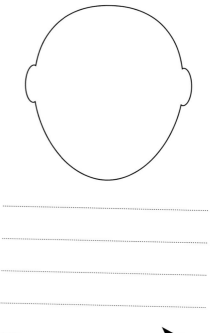

....

....

....

....

....

What happened next?

Mary and Joseph arrived at the temple with the baby Jesus, and Simeon was there watching. As soon as he could, the old man took the baby in his arms. He knew deep inside that this was the one he'd been waiting for. God was clearly letting Simeon know what to do and what to say! Here's what happened after that:

- Simeon gave thanks to God that the child he had been waiting all his life to see was there at last.
- Mary and Joseph looked on a little bit puzzled by the whole thing!
- Simeon prayed for Mary and Joseph.
- He told them that Jesus was an amazing sign and gift from God.
- He warned them that they would face sorrow and sadness.

I'm not sure how I would have felt if I'd been Mary and Joseph in this situation! Here's this old guy going nuts over their baby, and then telling them that he'd be great but they would suffer pain through it!

Waiting can be really hard to do. Simeon waited all his life to see the baby Jesus. What do people have to wait for? Use these letters to work out what we wait for.

R A N T I

— — — — —

M A L E Y P I T

— — — — — — —

Y O D A H I L

— — — — — — —

H I B T Y A D R

— — — — — — — —

S W E E D R A N   P A R R E Y

— — — — — —

— — — — —

How much hero?

Length of life

Really old and ready to die!   **85%**

Family

No info   **80%**

Amazing moments

Waiting, and seeing Jesus at last   **92%**

Doing God's stuff

Praying and then saying
what God led him to   **90%**

Generosity

Cared about Jesus and his parents   **80%**

Strength

Waited all his life   **90%**

TOTAL HERO RATING   86.1%

This story about Simeon is in Luke
2:22–35, and it's a great one!

Simeon had prayed and waited. He had heard God telling him to wait, and promising him that he really, really would see the Saviour, the Messiah, the gift from God. He was led by God to pray for the child and his mum and dad, to encourage them and to warn them. We don't know what happened to him after this moment, but I guess he quietly died in peace and happiness. He'd had to wait a long time, but at last his patience and prayer paid off. What a great old man, and what a hero!

Hero challenge

How are you at waiting? Think about times you have been impatient and had a go at others because of it. Next time, what could you do differently?

Jesus
The ultimate hero

Place	Galilee and Samaria
When	2,000 years ago
Job	Promised Messiah, teacher, leader, Son of God
Key bit	All of the life of Jesus!
Other guys	Disciples, Mary, Joseph, King Herod, Pilate

What do you think Jesus looked like? Draw him here.

Jesus is the ultimate hero! He was sent by the Father God to the world to make it possible for all people to be forgiven by God. God realised that the world was getting bad, and the only way to get it right again was to send his only Son to become a fully human boy and man, and to face up to the biggest battle ever – the battle over death! The coming of Jesus was given to God's messengers like Isaiah and Micah hundreds of years before, and Jesus did all that they thought he would. It's all a bit complicated, but God knew what he was doing!

Put these in order:

Jesus was born, and visited by wise men and shepherds.

Jesus was 12 when he was found talking about faith with the priests

Hundreds of years before, prophets and messengers said Jesus would come.

Jesus grew up with his parents, his dad Joseph was a carpenter.

An angel told Mary she would be having a VERY special baby.

Jesus was around 30 when it was the right time for him to do the real work that he had come to do. As a real man, he knew what it was like to be tempted because he spent 40 days in a wild place without food and water. He allowed his cousin John the Baptist to baptise him, and at that moment the clouds in the sky opened and God the Father spoke of his love for his son. Jesus then went on to call people to live a different way. He chose some disciples, special friends to work with him, and then travelled around the area doing really amazing things.

Can you link some of these amazing miracles and sayings of Jesus? Have a go, drawing a line to connect them:

Turned water	back to life
Said 'Love your neighbour	unable to walk
Brought a girl	and the life'
Said 'I am the way, the truth,	in the middle of a storm
Welcomed children to	come and talk to him
Fed 5,000 people	with a tiny amount of food
Told his friends to go out	given to you'
Said 'Ask, and it will be	and tell people about Jesus
Healed people who were	until the end of time'
Rode a donkey into the	as yourself'
Said 'I will be with you	into wine
Told the wind and waves to stop	city of Jerusalem

As Jesus did all those amazing miracles and said those brilliant things, he also knew that he would have to face a really horrible death. The religious leaders didn't like Jesus because he was popular, and said good things. The Romans, who were in charge of the land at that time, thought Jesus might get an army together and challenge their power. Jesus didn't go along with the crowd – he was brave, strong, and different. By the time Jesus had a special meal one evening with his friends Jesus knew that he would soon be hung on a cross. That same night he was arrested, beaten, spat at, had a crown made of huge, sharp thorns put on his head, and then told to drag part of the cross of heavy wood that he would hang on up a hill.

Would you have bottled out?

How much hero?

Length of life

33 years on earth, for ever in heaven   **100%**

Family

Mother Mary, human father Joseph   **100%**

Amazing moments

Birth, life, death and coming
alive again   **100%**

Doing God's stuff

Part of God himself, so did
brilliant work!   **100%**

Generosity

Came and died for everyone ever!   **100%**

Strength

Took all our bad onto the cross
and died   **100%**

TOTAL HERO RATING   100%

None of us can really imagine the pain of being nailed to a cross, the nails ripping through wrists and ankles. We can't hope to know what it's like to gradually lose the energy to hold your head up, and to finally not be able to breathe. Just to make sure that he had died, a soldier stabbed him in the side with a long sword. Jesus wasn't just a guy, he was the Son of God, yet he was killed in such a foul way! But that wasn't the end, and three days later Jesus left the cave where his body had been put, and was fully alive again. Evil hadn't won — Jesus had beaten death, and now lives on in heaven with Father God.

Jesus lived differently and challenged others to do the same. He faced up to a terrible time, yet still loves us and invites us to follow him and live as he did. Only real heroes follow Jesus, the ultimate hero!

Boy with lunch

A massive meal...

BACKGROUND BIT

Place	Hillside next to Lake Galilee
When	When Jesus was 30, 2,000 years ago
Job	Probably helping at home
Key bit	"There is a boy here who has five small loaves of barley bread and two fish." *John 6:9*
Other guys	Disciples, Philip, Andrew, Jesus

Write your own favourite packed lunch here:

....

....

....

....

....

Tick any of the following packed lunches you'd say were yummy and a cross against those you'd say were "yuck".

☐ Cheese and jam sandwiches

☐ Vegetable samosas and sheep's eyeballs

☐ Peanut butter and jam roll

☐ Banana and chocolate spread wrap

☐ Worm and mustard sandwich

☐ Sausage roll with snot pickle

☐ Bacon, lettuce and tomato sandwich

☐ Tuna mayo and liver sandwich

☐ Frogs' legs and cucumber sandwiches

☐ Cornish pasty

The friends of Jesus, his disciples, had a huge problem and a huge crowd! Thousands of people had turned out to hear Jesus speak on a hillside and they'd been there ages. No one seemed to want to go home, and as the day went on the disciples realised that lunchtime had come and they'd got no food for the crowd.

Look at all these hungry people...there must be thousands!

Where can we get enough food from?

It'll cost far too much

No Mum – just want to see that Jesus again, I'll be home before dark.

Here's some bread and fish for your lunch. Don't stay out too late!

There was a boy whose name we don't know, and that morning he'd joined the crowd to see and listen to Jesus. His lunch – five small loaves of bread and two fish – was wrapped up safe until he felt hungry.

As the disciples looked around, wondering what to do about the problem of feeding 5,000 or more, one of them called Andrew spotted the boy and his lunch. Before long the boy found that he'd handed his lunch over, and Jesus himself was praying over it. Then it was broken into bits, and shared out....and shared out...and shared out!

The boy watched with Jesus' friends as every person in the crowd ate plenty, and there were 12 baskets of food left over. Jesus had done a great thing – an incredible miracle. People in the crowd were amazed...and very full of fish and bread!

But the boy had done a great thing too, because without his lunch the people would have gone hungry.

We don't really know much else about this hero boy. Have a go at writing what he might have been thinking at different points in the story:

When he was listening to Jesus...

When he handed his lunch over...

When he saw Jesus pray with his food...

When he saw all the people eat loads...

When he got home I guess he would have been really excited about what happened, and keen to tell anyone who would listen!

How much hero?

Length of life
Don't know...but he gets extra
points for being a boy hero! **75%**

Family
He probably had a mum and dad! **80%**

Amazing moments
Giving up his lunch for others **80%**

Doing God's stuff
Went to see Jesus, helped by giving **80%**

Generosity
Totally! **100%**

Strength
Decided to be generous, not selfish **80%**

TOTAL HERO RATING **82.5%**

This great and generous boy is
mentioned in John chapter 6, so look it
up!

That boy shared his lunch, even
though he didn't need to. Have
a think about these... could you
do any of them? These things
heroes do!

- Share some sweets with a
  friend who hasn't got any.
- Take your old clothes and
  pass them on to someone
  with less.
- Give your unwanted toys and
  games to a charity shop.
- Spend some of playtime with
  someone who hasn't got
  many friends.
- Help someone in class who
  struggles to do things you
  find easy to do.
- Give an adult at home a hug
  for no reason!

**Sharing and giving is tough. We've
all got special things that are
precious to us, and we wouldn't
want to give to anyone. Draw a
special thing of yours here:**

Time for a snack!

Ants on a Log

What you need:

- 2 celery sticks
- Paring knife
- Butter knife
- Cutting board
- Raisins
- Cream cheese or peanut butter

What you do:

1 Wash the celery and ask an adult to help you use the paring knife to cut it into four pieces (about five inches long) on the cutting board.

2 Spread cream cheese or peanut butter on the celery sticks with your butter knife.

3 Add raisins and voila! You've got ants on a log.

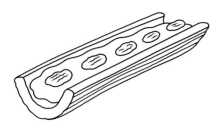

Personal Pizza

What you need:

- Whole wheat pitta bread
- Cheese slices
- Cherry tomatoes or tomato slices
- Microwave-safe plate
- Paring knife

What you do:

1 Place your pitta bread on the plate.

2 Add the cheese slices and tomatoes to the pitta.

3 Put the plate inside the microwave and close it shut. Set it for 30 seconds. (Parents may need to help here.)

4 Cut the pizza into four slices and it's ready!

Banana dog in a bun

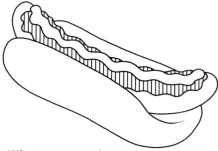

What you need:
- 1 hot dog bun (whole wheat, if possible)
- 1 tbsp peanut butter (or cream cheese)
- 1 tbsp strawberry or other jam (or honey, if preferred)
- 1 whole banana
- raisins, shredded coconut or chopped peanuts

What you do:
1 Spread one inner surface of a split hot dog bun with peanut butter or cream cheese. Spread the other side with jam or honey.
2 Put the banana in the bun, sprinkle on the toppings and eat.

Crispy rice apples

What you need:
- 3 tbsp honey
- 120g crispy rice cereal
- 1 apple

What you do:
1 Place honey and cereal into separate small bowls.
2 Cut apples into bite-size pieces, then stick the pieces with toothpicks.
3 Dip each apple piece in honey, then roll in cereal to coat. Enjoy!

A quick look at
Jairus

Who was he?
Jairus was an important guy who worked at a synagogue, a place where Jews worshipped God.

What did he do?
The people who were leaders in the synagogues didn't like Jesus, didn't trust Jesus, and didn't want anything to do with Jesus! But Jairus knew in his heart that Jesus was special, and when his 12-year-old daughter was ill he went rushing to Jesus and begged him to help.

What did Jesus do?
Jesus went to help a short while later, but by then the girl was dead. Jesus knew that Jairus had real faith, and the girl was healed, came alive, and brought great joy to loads of people.

What would you do?
You're not supposed to think Jesus is any good, but you know he can help you. Would you...

☐ Stay at home and watch your daughter die

☐ Go to Jesus and ask for help

☐ Try to see Jesus, but give up because of what others will say

Why a hero?
Jairus was not expected to have anything to do with Jesus, but he was a brave guy and a great dad! He knew Jesus could help, so despite what others thought he asked for help. That's a hero thing to do!

How much hero?

Look up the Bible passages about Jairus below and decide on the hero rating for each.

Length of life Doesn't say	☐ %
Family Luke 8:42	☐ %
Amazing moments Luke 8:56	☐ %
Doing God's stuff Luke 8:50–51	☐ %
Generosity Luke 8:43–49	☐ %
Strength Luke 8:49	☐ %
TOTAL HERO RATING	☐ %

Bartimaeus
Blind man who saw Jesus

BACKGROUND BIT

Place	Jericho, a really busy town
When	2,000 years ago
Job	Unable to work, so a beggar at the side of the road
Key bit	Jesus told him, "...Your eyes are healed because of your faith." *Mark 10:52*
Other guys	Jesus, the disciples, and a huge crowd

Most of us find it really tough to think about what it must be like to be blind. We like to see things, we get loads of pleasure in watching TV or DVDs, we love to play games on screens...

What things would you miss if you couldn't see them? Any of these?

Any other things? Draw them here.

Bart was blind. He lived at a time when there was no help. There were no white sticks, no gadgets and computers, and no trained dogs to guide him. He was unable to go to work to earn money. Now, that shouldn't have been a problem, because if people followed the law of the time they would have looked after Bart and everyone like him...but they didn't!

Bart heard a load of noise going on around him – there was a buzz in the air and something was going on, but he couldn't see what!

Bart was brave, determined, and wise. Despite the fact that he couldn't see Jesus, he knew that he was no ordinary guy – he called Jesus 'the Son of David'. This showed that Bart new his Old Testament! He knew that the promised Messiah, the true Son of God, would be a great–great–great (and so on!) son of King David. Bart shouted out louder, but that wasn't a popular move...

WHAT'S GOING ON?

BE QUIET!

Jesus heard Bart and called him over, while the crowd stood watching, like someone had pressed their pause button! Jesus asked Bart what he wanted, and his reply was pretty obvious really...

> *I want to see again.*

Bart knew that Jesus was special, and Jesus knew that Bart understood who he really was. Bart was full of faith, and because of that he was suddenly, dramatically and amazingly able to see again! Jesus had healed him and the crowd couldn't argue with that – they had seen and heard blind Bart day in and day out for years; now they saw him changed completely.

Blind people read through touch by using a special alphabet called Braille. This uses a series of raised dots to form letters and words. Use the Braille alphabet below to work out what Jesus said to Bartimaeus after he'd healed him.

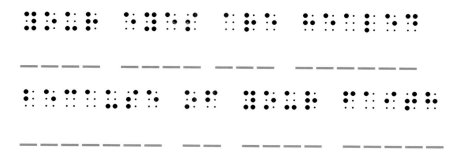

_____   _____   _____   _____

_____   ___   _____   _____

codebreaker

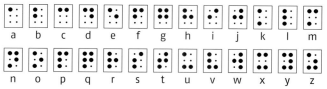

Bart knew the truth about Jesus, and wasn't scared to say it. The crowd told him to shut up, and he could easily have given up, but he didn't. Speaking out is tough, and this brave blind man becomes a hero for it – go Bart!

When do you have to speak out for Jesus? Are there times when you should, but you don't? Jot them here

....

....

....

....

....

....

....

....

....

....

How much hero?

Length of life
We don't really know   **70%**

Family
Son of Timaeus   **75%**

Amazing moments
Being healed of his blindness   **80%**

Doing God's stuff
Saw who Jesus was and
shouted it out!   **90%**

Generosity
Became a follower of Jesus   **80%**

Strength
Spoke out the truth in a tough place!   **85%**

TOTAL HERO RATING	80%

Read up on Bart's short and important story in Mark 10

Thomas

Asking the tough questions

BACKGROUND BIT

Place	Galilee, Judea, wherever Jesus went
When	Nearly 2,000 years ago
Job	Friend of Jesus
Key bit	"Thomas replied, 'You are my Lord and my God!'" *John 20:28*
Other guys	All the other disciples, Jesus

There's nothing wrong with asking questions! When you were younger you'll probably have gone through a time when all you ever did was ask questions and say "Why?" to lots of things! Ask those who were around and see what they say! Here are some questions that lots of people ask:

IF GOD MADE EVERYTHING, WHO MADE GOD?

Where do odd socks go (apart from under your bed!)?

Why is the world round?

Can we see God?

Why is there suffering in the world?

Write down any questions you have in your mind

....

....

....

....

Thomas was one of the disciples right from the beginning. When Jesus chose the 12 special friends who would be with him and help him in all that he had to do, he saw in Thomas something that he needed. Through some of the things that happened to Jesus and his mates we learn a few things about Thomas, and why he should be thought of as a hero.

Brave

? What does brave mean? Are you brave?

Thomas was a brave guy! Jesus and the disciples had travelled through Bethany, and the people there hadn't liked Jesus much. In fact, they hated him so much that they had threatened to throw stones at him to kill him! But when Jesus heard that his friend Lazarus back in Bethany had died, he planned to go back to help. What do you think the disciples said?

Oh great – it'll be fun to dodge those stones!

We can't go back there – it's a bit cold

Go back...but they tried to stone you!

Thomas was the sort of man who asked questions and thought about things. He knew the risks of going back, but he calmly suggested that they all went.

Thinker

? Do you know people who think a lot? Who are they?

Thomas always listened really carefully to what Jesus said and tried to understand it, but that wasn't always easy because Jesus sometimes used stories and strange descriptions to explain stuff. So when Jesus was talking with his friends one day about how he would die and go to another place, Thomas wanted to know where that place was so he could go there too! He didn't quite get that Jesus meant heaven. Thomas asked the questions that needed asking, but the others didn't think of.

Checker

? Does anyone you know check things lots? Do they write lists?

What happened next?

- Thomas was there when Jesus was arrested and he watched Jesus die on the cross.
- When Jesus came alive again and went to see his friends Thomas was not there.
- When his friends told him how Jesus was alive he wasn't able to be sure. He wanted to check out their story – he wanted to see Jesus himself.
- A week later, Jesus was suddenly in the room, and invited Thomas to put his fingers in the nail holes on his hands, and put his hand into the sword gash in his side.
- We don't know whether Thomas did... seeing Jesus was enough for it to check out!

Are you a checker or a believer? Circle which of these choices you would do? Results at foot of page.

1 You're told that playtime is going to go on longer than normal. Would you:

  A Carry on playing.
  B Go and check with the teacher?

2 You get a letter in an envelope from school to take home to your parents. Would you:

  A Take it home as it is.
  B Open it and read it first?

3 Your brother or sister tells you you're in trouble! Would you:

  A Keep out of the way and hope!
  B Go and find out why you're in trouble?

I think God wants his heroes to be a bit of both!
All B – you're a checker, and like to know the facts.
All A – you're a believer, and just get on with life.

Thomas is often called "Doubting Thomas", because he doubted that Jesus had come alive again. Faith is important, and we can't always check and prove things we believe in. But really I think he's Thinking Thomas, and there's nothing wrong with that! God gave us all brains, although some of us don't use them as much as we could! Thomas shows that thinking things through, asking tough questions and only trusting what you're really sure of, are good things to do. So in my mind he's a hero!

Can you unravel this spaghetti to work out what it says?

How much hero?

Length of life
A good life serving God — **80%**

Family
Called 'the twin' — **75%**

Amazing moments
Seeing Jesus' scars for himself — **90%**

Doing God's stuff
A brave disciple but could
have trusted more — **75%**

Generosity
Gave his life to serve Jesus — **90%**

Strength
Used his brain, asked questions — **90%**

TOTAL HERO RATING	83.3%

Thomas is mentioned in the gospels (Matthew, Mark, Luke, John), and the bit about him seeing Jesus is John 20:24–29.

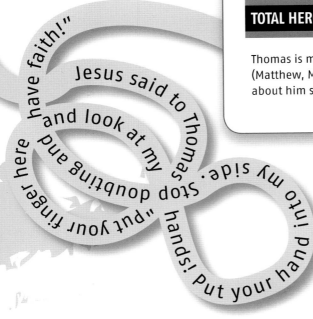

Jesus said to Thomas. Stop doubting and have faith!" "Put your finger here and look at my hands! Put your hand into my side.

Zacchaeus

How much hero?

Look up the Bible passages about Zacchaeus below and decide on the hero rating for each.

Length of life
Doesn't say
[ ] %

Family
Doesn't say
[ ] %

Amazing moments
Luke 19:4,9
[ ] %

Doing God's stuff
Luke 19:6
[ ] %

Generosity
Luke 19:8
[ ] %

Strength
Luke 19:7
[ ] %

TOTAL HERO RATING [ ] %

Why a hero?
Zac was no hero at the start, but he was willing to change everything, ask for people to forgive him again, and put the wrong things right. That's pretty brave stuff.

Who was he?
Zac was a tax collector who cheated the people in his area. He took more money than he should have and kept loads for himself.

What did he do?
Zac heard that Jesus was visiting his village and wanted to see him. But Zac was only a little guy, so he climbed a tree to watch.

What did Jesus do?
Jesus stopped in the middle of the crowd and looked up to see Zac. He called him down, went to his house, and talked with him. Zac was so convinced that Jesus was something else that he promised to give money to the poor and pay loads extra back to those he had cheated.

What would you do?
You've made a lot of money out of cheating people, but now you've met Jesus you know you've done wrong. Would you...

[ ] Give back all the money and more to everyone

[ ] Move away from that village

[ ] Give a little to everyone, but keep as much as you can

Peter
Go for it whatever!

BACKGROUND BIT

Place	Capernaum, Lake Galilee, lots of travels too
When	At the time of Jesus
Job	Fisherman, disciple, preacher
Key bit	"So I will call you Peter, which means 'a rock'. On this rock I will build my church." *Matthew 16:18*
Other guys	Brother Andrew, all the disciples, lots of other people

Peter was a fisherman when Jesus came along and asked him to join him. Peter, then called Simon, didn't hesitate, and left his boat where it was. He travelled around with Jesus, and sometimes used the boat to travel across the big Lake Galilee.

One day Peter and his friend were crossing the lake when a big wind blew up, and a storm followed. The storm lasted most of the night...

What would you do?
- [ ] Shout for help
- [ ] Jump from the boat
- [ ] Give up and cry!

Early in the morning Peter and the others saw a figure walking towards them across the water, and they were pretty scared. Some of them shouted and screamed with fear! But Jesus called to them and explained that it was him, telling them not to be so afraid.

What would you do?
- [ ] Continue being scared
- [ ] Wave to Jesus
- [ ] Check that you're not dreaming!

What would you do?
- [ ] Move away from Jesus
- [ ] Say 'Wow!'
- [ ] Worship him

Peter really trusted Jesus, and instantly stepped from the boat. He kept looking at Jesus while he walked over the water just like he'd seen Jesus do. But then his eyes wandered to the big waves, and he got scared and started to sink. Jesus was watching, and reached out to Peter, teasing him about not having enough faith! Jesus and Peter got back into the boat and the wind died down.

BIBLE HEROES

Lots of people think Peter is a hero, simply because he was a bit of a disaster area too! Here are some of the other key moments from the life of Peter:

- Peter was a fisherman when Jesus came along and asked him to join him. Peter, then called Simon, didn't hesitate, and left his boat where it was.
- Peter was a bit quick to speak out or jump into action. He was with Jesus at some great moments, like when Jesus was on a boat and stopped a huge storm.
- Jesus was arrested late at night by some guards working for the temple leaders, and Peter was so angry that he grabbed a sword and cut one of the guards' ears off, leaving blood everywhere!
- Just before he was arrested Peter promised Jesus that he would never leave him and he'd always be on Jesus' side, but early the next morning Peter told some strangers that he didn't even know Jesus.

Have you ever said something and wished you could get hold of the words and put them back into your mouth? What happened?

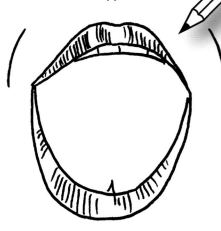

Peter saw Jesus again after he had been crucified and had come alive again, and then Jesus forgave Peter for denying him. Then Jesus made sure Peter really loved him, before asking Peter to be the main man in starting the church.

What happened next?

- Peter was there when Jesus went up to heaven, and when the Holy Spirit came.
- Peter became an amazing preacher, and changed lives through what he said.
- He was thrown into prison, but angels lead him out past sleeping guards and through locked doors!
- He learned more from God as he got older, and realised that Jesus came to be friends with all people.
- It's thought that he died in Rome, where he was put on a cross and hung upside-down until he couldn't breathe and had bled to death.

An angel helped Peter escape from prison. Follow the path he used to lead Peter to safety.

How much hero?

Length of life
9omewhere around 70, nasty death   **80%**

Family
Brother was Andrew, dad Jonah   **85%**

Amazing moments
Following Jesus, the storm,
Jesus alive again   **100%**

Doing God's stuff
Became a loyal follower and
a great preacher   **85%**

Generosity
Would do anything for Jesus   **93%**

Strength
Strong, energetic, determined   **80%**

TOTAL HERO RATING   87.1%

Peter is written about in the gospels
(Matthew, Mark, Luke, John), and Acts.
He's worth looking up.

All through his life Peter had a habit of jumping in and doing things before he'd thought them through, and this got him into bother! He was a follower who failed from time to time, but we fail too. So we, like Peter, can go for it and be heroes!

Peter was really upset with himself when he denied knowing Jesus, and said sorry as soon as he could. Jesus forgave him, and forgives us too.

Have a think – are there any things you feel really sorry for that you've never asked Jesus to forgive?

Save me!

When Peter stepped into the water and had his eyes on Jesus he was able to walk, but as soon as he looked away he started to sink! Look it up in the Bible – Matthew 14:30.

Peter simply prayed "Lord, save me!" We can do the same – we don't need to use lots of complicated words to reach out to Jesus and ask for help – a few words in stressful times will do!

Fill out these simple prayers for help, thinking of times in life, at home, or at school when you need that little extra that Jesus offers! Remember these quick prayers so that when you're in a tough place you can pray simply and powerfully!

Lord, save me when...

....

Lord, help me say the right things when...

....

Lord, give me patience when...

....

Lord, give me peace when...

....

Lord, help me understand when....

....

Lord, give me amazing strength when...

....

A quick look at
Paul

How much hero?

Look up the Bible passages about Paul below and decide on the hero rating for each.

Length of life

Not known, but he was quite old by the time he died — [ ] %

Family

Not known — [ ] %

Amazing moments

Acts 9:3-6 — [ ] %

Doing God's stuff

Acts 16:16+ — [ ] %

Generosity

Acts 19 — [ ] %

Strength

Acts 22 — [ ] %

TOTAL HERO RATING [ ] %

Why a hero?

Paul was one of the first great leaders of the Christian church, and without him many of the first churches wouldn't have started. He was brave, fearless, and really trusted God.

Who was he?

Paul was originally called Saul and was an enemy of Christians.

What did he do?

Saul did all he could to get Christians punished for following Jesus, but then he had an amazing experience. He was travelling along a road when a blinding light stopped him in his tracks, and the voice of Jesus spoke to him. From then on Saul changed his name to Paul, and instead of attacking Christians he became one of them.

Paul travelled to many places telling people about Jesus, and helping churches start.

What did God do?

God changed Paul's life around. He gave Paul loads of good gifts like speaking, preaching and writing.

What would you do?

You have been arrested for being a follower of Jesus, and you are brought before the king who has the power to have you killed. Would you:

- [ ] Be worried and lost for words
- [ ] Say sorry and beg to be forgiven and released
- [ ] Speak out and tell the king all about Jesus

A quick look at
Stephen

Who was he?
Stephen was one of the first people to start setting up churches and talking about Jesus after Jesus had returned to heaven.

What did he do?
Stephen was a great preacher, and really stood up for the truth of Jesus. He was arrested because of it, and questioned by lots of serious religious people who didn't understand that God sent Jesus for everyone. As Stephen spoke about how they should have listened to Jesus, they got really angry, dragged him outside, and then threw stones at him.

What did God do?
God gave Stephen the strength to speak out without being afraid, to endure the horrible pain of this slow death, and still to ask God to help those nasty people.

What would you do?
Like Stephen, you're up in front of loads of serious men who totally disagree with you. Would you:

- [ ] Start to speak, then give up and sit down
- [ ] Go for it with God's guidance, and face whatever comes
- [ ] Agree that you'd got it wrong, and split!

How much hero?

Look up the Bible passages about Stephen below and decide on the hero rating for each.

Length of life
Not known but cut short by being stoned to death
[ ] %

Family
Not known
[ ] %

Amazing moments
Acts 6:8
[ ] %

Doing God's stuff
Acts 6:10
[ ] %

Generosity
Acts 7:59–60
[ ] %

Strength
Acts 7:54–56
[ ] %

TOTAL HERO RATING [ ] %

Why a hero?
Stephen was the first person to die for trusting Jesus and speaking about him. He wasn't scared, he kept telling the truth, and he faced death calmly and full of God.

Barnabus
Risk-taker and church-maker

BACKGROUND BIT

Place	Jerusalem, Cyprus, and towns where churches were starting
When	A few years after Jesus' death
Job	Teacher, encourager
Key bit	"Then Barnabus helped him by taking him to the apostles." Acts 9:27
Other guys	All the disciples, Saul (who became Paul), Mark

What would you think if the boy in your class at school that you really don't get on with started to be nice to you? How would you feel if he wanted to be involved in everything you like to do? Would you...

☐ Trust him and welcome him

☐ Be a bit puzzled but go along with it

☐ Treat him suspiciously

☐ Ignore him

☐ Tell him to go away and leave you alone

Barnabus was a wise guy, a real risk-taker, and probably the key to loads of things that happened when the Christian faith started. At that time many new Christians feared Saul because he worked hard to pick on them (see page 86). Saul approved of Stephen being killed by a crowd throwing stones at him!

As we've already seen, Saul was dramatically changed by God and became known as Paul, and started to preach about Jesus. He was really successful and loads of people started new churches because of him. But the other church leaders, people like Peter and the other disciples, weren't so sure about Saul. Had he really changed? Was he a spy trying to trick them? That's when Barnabus took a BIG risk...

Have you ever taken a BIG risk? Was it a terrific triumph or a dreadful disaster? Write or draw about it here.

What happened next?

- Barnabus brought Paul to Jerusalem to all the disciples, and persuaded them Paul was now a true Christian.
- Paul went on to be a super-hero, and thousands of people found out all about Jesus because of him.
- Barnabus travelled with Paul and lots of new churches were set up.
- Barnabus encouraged a younger man, John Mark, to go with them and help, but Paul wasn't so keen.
- Barnabus took the risk with John Mark, and he turned out to be a really good guy... and even went on to write Mark's Gospel.

Barnabus was known as "Mr Encouragement" because he loved to help people and get them to do things they never knew they could do!

Decode this message to find out what the Bible says about Barnabus in Acts 11:24

codebreaker

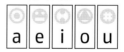

a e i o u

B o rn a b a s w a s o g oo d m a n
o f gr e a t f oo th, o nd h e
w a s f i ll e d w i th th e H o ly
Sp i r i t. M o ny m o r e p e o pl e
t o rn e d t o th e L o rd w i th
o ll th e o r h e o rts.

It is loads easier to criticise someone and say harsh things than it is to encourage and build them up. That's why Barnabus is different – all he did was about getting people to do more by making them feel good about themselves. Without him Paul might not have been accepted as a great teacher and preacher, and the Gospel of Mark may never have been written. That's pretty great work, Barnabus!

What things do you say to others? What things do people say to you? Circle the encouraging ones that make you feel good, and put a cross over the ones that make you feel fed up:

How much hero?

Length of life
He served God for many years — **80%**

Family
Sister – Mary — **70%**

Amazing moments
Getting Paul accepted by the apostles — **80%**

Doing God's stuff
Told people about Jesus, encouraged everyone! — **85%**

Generosity
Gave all he could to others — **100%**

Strength
Took risks that could have gone bad! — **90%**

TOTAL HERO RATING **84.1%**

Barnabus pops up loads of times in the New Testament. Main bits include Acts 4:36, Acts 9, and lots of Acts 11–15.

Is that the best you can do?

That's great!

Go on – do your best

Well done – I'm well impressed.

You can do it

I don't think you'll be any good.

That was rubbish

Hero signs

Trust

Many of the heroes in the Bible are real heroes because they really trusted God. Even though they went through tough times or faced massive battles, they had no doubt that God was on their side, and he would help them. Many of them also trusted other people like family and friends, and that helped them.

So who do you trust? Write their names and draw them in the outlines.

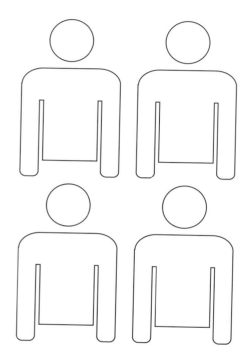

BIG QUESTION Do you trust God?

☐ YES   ☐ NO

Fearless

These hero boys and men knew that they were going to battle, to speak out a message that people hated, or even to their death, yet their fear didn't stop them. It's normal to be a bit afraid, but that doesn't stop us facing up to challenges and tough tasks. God makes us calm, and able to do the stuff.

BIG QUESTION Are you scared to speak out for God?

☐ YES   ☐ NO

When have you been scared?

Young

Quite a lot of Bible heroes are old, and many learned how to be heroes as they got older. But some started out at your age or even younger, and were heroes from the start. They listened to God, loved to live on the edge, and stood up against the bad guys. You are just the sort of boy that God wants to be his hero NOW, not just when you're old and mouldy!

GOD'S HERO

▲ **Draw yourself here**

Sorry

It's not a wimpy thing to do to say sorry when you've got it wrong. Many of our Bible heroes weren't perfect, and some made tons of mistakes. But they all knew that God would forgive and help if they said sorry and meant it. Heroes know their own mistakes, and know that "sorry" is an important word.

God, thank you that you forgive. I'm sorry for...

Finish the sentence above.

Listener

These Bible heroes were all led by God to live bravely and stand up for what's right. God spoke to them in loads of different ways, and they not only heard him but they listened carefully. God wants to make you a hero, and could speak to you through others, through the Bible, and through how you feel inside.

To listen you need to be quiet. Where are you quiet to listen to God?

How much hero?

Add up the six numbers and divide them by 6 for *your* total hero rating.

Length of life		%
Family		%
Amazing moments		%
Doing God's stuff		%
Generosity		%
Strength		%
TOTAL HERO RATING		%

Honest

You can't be a hero and tell lies all the time! Our Bible heroes were honest boys and men most of the time, even though some of them went a bit wrong. When we lie we are only thinking of protecting ourselves, and can't face up to what we do. Heroes are honest.

X

And so...

These are just some of the boys and men from the Bible that are heroes. Some spoke out, some fought battles, some helped others and some were leaders. YOU can be a hero for God too... it's all about being different, and listening to God speak to you through others, through the Bible, and through how you feel inside. Being a hero is the tough option – it's dead easy to go along with the crowd. Anyone can swear with their mates, hurt others, lie, or cheat. It takes a strong, brave hero to do the right thing and stick with it. So are you up for it? Can you face the ultimate challenge? Have a go at your own TOTAL HERO RATING.

Answers

Page 9 Spot the difference

Page 10 Alphabet code: sweets

Page 11 Matching things: Sky – Moon; Sea – Boat; Head – Hat; Coffee – Mug/Cup; Foot – Shoe; Game controller – Game console; Books – School bag; Neck – Tie; Fish – Chips; Car – Road

Page 26 Rubble maze

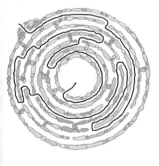

Page 44 Joash's story: D, B, E, F, A, C

Page 50 Isaiah's prophecies: A young woman is pregnant, she will have a son and name him Emmanuel – Mary gave birth to Jesus, and Emmanuel means "God with us"; He was wounded and crushed for our sins – Jesus was wounded and then put on the cross; He was painfully abused, but did not complain – Jesus was arrested and then beaten and abused; He was condemned to death without a fair trial – None of the important people knew what to do with Jesus, so they asked the people, who shouted "Crucify him!"

Page 53 Food wordsearch

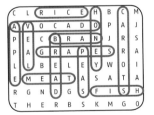

Page 59 Things we wait for: Train, Playtime, Holiday, Birthday, Answered prayer

Page 63 Miracles and sayings: Turned water – into wine; Said 'Love your neighbour – as yourself'; Brought a girl – back to life; Said 'I am the way, the truth, – and the life'; Welcomed children to – come and talk to him; Fed 5,000 people – with a tiny amount of food; Told his friends to go out – and tell people about Jesus; Said 'Ask, and it will be – given to you'; Healed people who were – unable to walk; Rode a donkey into the – city of Jerusalem; Said 'I will be with you – until the end of time'; Told the wind and waves to stop – in the middle of a storm

Page 62 Putting into order: 1 Hundreds of years before, prophets and messengers said Jesus would come. 2 An angel told Mary she would be having a VERY special baby. 3 Jesus was born, and visited by wise men and shepherds. 4 Jesus grew up with his parents, his dad Joseph was a carpenter. 5 Jesus was 12 when he was found talking about faith with the priests.

Page 74 Braille code: Your eyes are healed because of your faith

Page 79 Spaghetti verse: Jesus said to Thomas "Put your finger here and look at my hands! Put your hand into my side. Stop doubting and have faith!"

Page 83 Peter escapes

Page 90 Coded message: "Barnabus was a good man of great faith, and he was filled with the Holy Spirit. Many more people turned to the Lord with all their hearts"

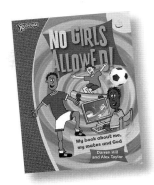

No Girls Allowed!

Alex Taylor and Darren Hill
This is a book about you and for you! Challenges, facts, puzzles – to do on your own or with your mates. Keep track of what and who you are. On the way you'll discover what God thinks of you and that he can be the best mate ever!

£4.99 ISBN 978 1 84427 209 9

Massive Prayer Adventure

Sarah Mayers
Make a fresh start in the way you talk with God. Discover loads about him and try out different ways of speaking and listening. You are in for surprise! Another must-read!

£4.99 ISBN 978 1 84427 211 2

SPACE INVADERS

Kathy Lee
Paul's life is going wrong. His mum has left and his dad is marrying someone with three children of her own. But when Paul and his annoying, space-obsessed half-brother see a UFO, Paul can think of nothing else. Will they discover the origins of the alien slime on the moors, and will Paul fight off his own Space Invaders?

£4.99 ISBN 978 1 84427 507 6